Apple Cid~~~~~~ar Rec.

45 Apple Cider Vinegar Recipes for Weight Loss

By: Kevin Kerr

Table of Contents

Introduction

You may have used apple cider vinegar for your homemade marinades, pickles and salad dressings before. It is definitely a tasty addition in your kitchen and the good news is that it is also good for your health.

Apple cider vinegar provides a wide range of health benefits, aside from the fact that it can aid in weight loss as well as help enhance your mood.

Going back to weight loss, apples are known to contain high amounts of an insoluble fiber referred to as pectin. When it comes to weight loss or healthy eating, it is crucial to consume high fiber food as they actually help in increasing feelings of both fullness and satisfaction. Since apple cider vinegar is basically made from apples, it then follows that it is high in pectin. It is even suggested that drinking a glass of water dissolved with 1 to 2 tablespoons of apple cider prior to eating can help you feel full, thus helps in controlling your food consumption.

Now how then does apple cider vinegar help enhance your mood? Since it helps to break down proteins into amino acids, these amino acids go on and fuel processes inside your body, with it the formation of hormones. And aside from that, amino acids are also the reason how tryptophan is created. Tryptophan plays an important role in the release of serotonin in your body, which is in fact referred to as one of your body's "feel good" neurotransmitters. It then elevates your mood and help lower down feelings of anxiety or even depression.

BLT Baked Mac and Cheese

Ingredients Needed:

- 8 oz of bacon
- 12 oz of macaroni
- 2 1/4 cups of milk
- 1/2 tsp of turmeric
- 6 oz of cream cheese
- 2 cups of cheddar cheese
- 6 oz of cherry tomatoes
- salt
- pepper
- 1/4 cup of Greek yogurt
- 1 tbsp of apple cider vinegar
- 2 romaine hearts

Directions:

1. Preheat oven: 375 °F.
2. Cook bacon till crisp; set aside.
3. Cook pasta in salted water. Drain.
4. Simmer milk. Add the turmeric. Stir in cream cheese, keep cooking till melted. Add cheddar cheese; let it melt. Throw in pasta, bacon and tomatoes. Stir and flavor using salt & pepper. Bake on a 9 by 13-inch pan for 20 minutes.
5. Combine vinegar and yogurt; whisk. Add lettuce, flavor using salt & pepper.

Serve alongside romaine salad.

Grilled Corn and Vidalia Onion Salad

Ingredients Needed:

- 5 corn ears
- ⅔ cups of Vidalia onion
- ⅔ cups of cherry tomatoes
- 1 tbsp of olive oil
- 1 tsp of lime juice
- 1 tsp of apple cider vinegar
- ¼ tsp of salt
- 1 tbsp of cilantro

Directions:

1. Combine tomatoes, olive oil, vinegar, corn kernels, lime juice, onions, and salt.
2. Sprinkle cilantro.

BBQ Sauce Smoked Chicken

Ingredients Needed:

- 6 pcs chicken

Barbecue sauce:

- 1 cup of ketchup
- 1 cup of honey
- 3 tbsp of molasses
- 2 tbsp of Worcestershire sauce
- 2 tsp of black pepper
- 1 tsp of white pepper
- 2 tsp of liquid smoke
- ¼ cup of apple cider vinegar

Directions:

1. Prep for BBQ sauce: combine all ingredients and blend. Bring to a boil using a saucepan.
2. Using hickory or apple, smoke chicken. Use the prepared BBQ sauce as basting and continue smoking for around 20 to 30 minutes.

Pulled Pork Sandwich

Ingredients Needed:

Pickled red onions:

- 1 tbsp of granulated sugar
- 1 tsp of salt
- 1/3 cup of apple cider vinegar
- ½ cup of hot water
- 1 red onion

Upstater sandwich:

- 6 oz of cream cheese
- 3 tbsp of maple syrup
- ¼ tsp of cayenne pepper
- 4 ciabatta rolls
- 2 apples
- 2 cups of smoked pork
- 1 cup of arugula

Directions:

Prep for pickled red onions:

1. Combine apple cider vinegar, hot water, sugar, and salt,
2. Keep stirring till salt and sugar is dissolved. Mix in the sliced onion; keep stirring. Leave for an hour.

Prep for Upstater sandwich:

1. Combine maple syrup, cayenne pepper, and cream cheese. Slather on all ciabatta rolls.
2. Use a mandolin to shave the apples thinly. Set aside.
3. Arrange pulled pork on bottom halves of rolls. Top with the sliced apples, fresh arugula and pickled onions.

Texas Caviar

Ingredients Needed:

- 2 cups of black beans
- 2 cups of black eyed peas
- 1 cup of red pepper
- 1 cup of green pepper
- 1/2 cup of red onion
- 2 onions
- 1 cup of corn
- 1 1/4 cup of cherry tomatoes
- 1 1/2 tbsp of lime juice
- 1 tbsp of olive oil
- 1 tbsp of apple cider vinegar
- salt

Directions:

Combine all ingredients together. Mix well.

Let sit overnight in fridge.

Vegan Banana Nut Muffins

Ingredients Needed:

- 1 tbsp of flax seed
- 3 tbsp of water
- 1 1/4 cups of soy milk
- 2 tsp of apple cider vinegar
- 2 cups of pastry flour
- 1/2 cup of coconut sugar
- 1 1/2 tsp of baking powder
- 1/2 tsp of baking soda
- 1/2 tsp of salt
- 3 tbsp of maple syrup
- 1 tsp of vanilla extract
- 2 bananas
- 1/2 cup of coconut
- 2/3 cup of walnuts

Directions:

1. Preheat oven: 350 °F. Line a muffin tin with paper liners or spray with nonstick cooking spray.
2. Combine the water and ground flax to make flax egg. Set aside to thicken.
3. Combine apple cider vinegar and soy milk. Set aside.
4. Combine sugar, baking soda, baking powder, flour, and salt. Stir in maple syrup, milk, vanilla extract then mashed bananas. Mix well. Add walnuts and coconut.
5. Place the batter onto 12 muffin tins.
6. Bake for around 15-17 minutes. Let cool before serving.
7. Leave in the fridge or store inside airtight containers.

Walnut & Chicken Salad with Blueberry Vinaigrette

Ingredients Needed:

Blueberry vinaigrette:

- 1/2 cup of blueberries
- 1 tbsp of honey
- 1 tbsp of apple cider vinegar
- 1 tsp of red wine vinegar
- 3/4 tsp of mustard
- salt
- pepper
- 1 tbsp of olive oil

Salad:

- 8 oz of chicken tenders
- 1 tbsp of vegetable oil
- 5-6 oz of romaine
- 2/3 cup of corn
- 1/4 cup of walnuts
- 4 leaves basil

Directions:

1. Using a food processor, blend together the vinegars, blueberries, honey, and mustard. Pour olive oil then add salt & pepper; pulse to combine.
2. Cook chicken tenders on a pan for 4 to 5 minutes each side. Slice into bite sized pieces.
3. Mix together romaine, corn, chicken, walnuts, and basil. Stir in blueberry vinaigrette then serve.

Spicy Tomato And Pepper Chutney

Ingredients Needed:

- 2 tomatoes
- 2 roma tomatoes
- 2 Italian peppers
- 2 Serrano peppers
- 2 tsp of sugar
- ⅛ tsp of pepper
- ⅛ tsp of red pepper flakes
- ⅛ tsp of salt
- 1 tsp of apple cider vinegar

Directions:

1. Combine all ingredients on a pan.
2. Let boil first and then lower down heat and simmer 40 minutes. The consistency of sauce is ideally thick and chunky.

Spicy Apple - Carrot Chutney

Ingredients Needed:

- 1 tbsp of coconut oil
- 1 red onion
- ¼ tsp of cumin
- ⅛ tsp of coriander
- ⅛ tsp of cardamom
- 1 tsp of black pepper
- ⅛ tsp of mustard powder
- ⅛ tsp of cinnamon
- ⅛ tsp of cloves
- ⅛ tsp of nutmeg
- ½ tsp of 5 spice powder
- ¼ tsp of red pepper flakes
- salt
- Schezuan peppercorns
- 1 tsp of gingerroot
- 2 garlic cloves
- 4 apples
- 1 carrot
- ½ cup of dark raisins
- ¼ cup of coconut
- 2 tbsp of raw sugar
- ¼ cup of xylitol
- ¼ cup of apple cider vinegar
- 1 cup of apple juice

Directions:

1. Melt coconut oil.
2. Sauté spices, ginger, onion, garlic for 15 minutes.
3. Stir in the carrots, coconut apples, raisins, xylitol, sugar, apple juice and apple cider vinegar

4. Let simmer: 20 minutes without a cover. Transfer to jars then place on a water bath for 20 mins.

Collard Green Salad

Ingredients Needed:

- 1 lb of collard greens
- 1 bell pepper
- 2 diced tomatoes
- 3 tbsp of olive oil
- ½ cup of apple cider vinegar
- 2 tbsp of soy sauce
- 1 tbsp of honey
- salt
- pepper

Directions:

1. Mix in olive oil with collard greens for 5 minutes.
2. Add in peppers.
3. Combine soy sauce, honey and vinegar; whisk. Drizzle on the peppers and greens; toss.
4. Leave in the fridge for 2 hours.
5. Add tomatoes before serving.
6. Flavor using pepper and salt.

Detox Salad

Ingredients Needed:

- 2 sweet potatoes
- 6 cups of kale
- 2 cups of red cabbage
- 1 squash
- ⅓ cup of tahini
- ⅓ cup of apple cider vinegar
- ⅓ cup of lemon juice
- 1 tbsp of honey
- 1 tbsp of ginger
- 1 clove garlic
- 2 tbsp of cilantro
- salt

Directions:

1. Bake the sweet potatoes.
2. Dice then leave in the fridge to cool.
3. Boil water.
4. Boil the kale for a minute then drain.
5. Leave kale in the fridge till cold.
6. Mix together vegetables, stirring in sweet potatoes without mashing.
7. Combine together the rest of the ingredients; whisk.
8. Drizzle over vegetables; toss well.

Dreamy Vegan Mushroom Stroganoff

Ingredients Needed:

- 1 package of fettuccini
- 2 Portobello mushrooms
- ½ cup of veggie broth
- ½ cup of almond
- 2 tbsp of apple cider vinegar
- 1 tbsp of nutritional yeast
- 1 tbsp of miso paste
- 2 tsp of soy sauce
- ½ tsp of nutmeg
- ½ tsp of cayenne pepper
- ¼ tsp of liquid smoke
- Salt
- pepper
- basil

Directions:

1. Slice mushrooms thinly.
2. Combine the liquid smoke, a teaspoon veggie broth and soy sauce; whisk. Stir in mushrooms and toss.
3. Let mushrooms marinate for 30 minutes.
4. Add the rest of ingredients minus the pasta with the mushrooms on a saucepan and let boil.
5. Simmer the sauce over low heat. Cook pasta.
6. Drain pasta and pour sauce, tossing well to combine.
7. Garnish with torn basil leaves.

Warm Potato Salad

Ingredients Needed:

- 2 1/2 lbs of Yukon gold
- 1 1/2 tsp of kosher salt
- 1 shallot
- 2 tbsp of spicy brown mustard
- 1 tbsp of apple cider vinegar
- 1/4 cup of olive oil
- 1 tsp of black pepper
- 1 red pepper
- 2 tbsp of flat leaf parsley

Directions:

1. Place potatoes in a saucepan and add cold water.
2. Let boil after adding a teaspoon kosher salt. When boiling, simmer over low heat for 10 minutes.
3. Drain and leave to cool down.
4. Combine brown mustard, shallots, apple cider vinegar, half-teaspoon kosher salt then ground black pepper; whisk.
5. While whisking, add in olive oil and emulsify.
6. Mix in the potatoes with the parsley and red peppers.
7. Toss well.

Creamy Poppy Seed Dressing

Ingredients Needed:

- 1 tbsp of poppy seeds
- 1 tbsp of honey
- 8 oz of Greek yogurt, plain
- 1 tbsp of apple cider vinegar
- 1 tbsp of orange juice
- salt
- pepper

Directions:

1. Mix together all ingredients.
2. Season according to your taste.
3. Leave in the refrigerator.

Southern Deviled Eggs

Ingredients Needed:

- 6 eggs
- 3 tbsp of mayonnaise
- 1/2 tsp of mustard
- 1 tsp of apple cider vinegar
- tbsp of sweet relish
- salt
- pepper
- paprika

Directions:

1. Halve lengthwise each boiled then peeled eggs. Take out yolks and mash using a fork. Stir in mustard, mayonnaise, pickle relish, salt & pepper. Combine well.
2. Fill each egg with at least a teaspoon of yolk mixture.
3. Sprinkle with paprika.

Potato Salad with Cornichons and Radishes

Ingredients Needed:

Salad:

- 2 lbs of potatoes
- 7 oz of cornichons
- 1 bunch radishes
- ⅓ cup of chives
- 1 red onion

Vinaigrette:

- ⅓ cup of neutral oil
- tbsp of mustard
- 2 tbsp of Dijon mustard
- ⅓ cup of apple cider vinegar
- Salt
- pepper

Directions:

1 Combine all salad ingredients.
2 Put all vinaigrette ingredients in a jar and shake well. Drizzle over the salad then serve.

Goat Cheese Stuffed Bacon, Peach & Basil Burgers

Ingredients Needed:

Burgers:

- 1 lb. ground beef
- tbsp of bell pepper
- 1/2 tsp of chili powder
- 1 oz of goat cheese
- salt
- pepper

Peach chutney:

- 2 thick bacon slices
- 1/2 onion
- 1 garlic clove
- 1/2 cup of peach preserves
- 1 tbsp of apple cider vinegar
- 1/2 tsp of chili powder
- 1/4 tsp of ginger

Serving:

- hamburger buns
- 1 peach
- basil leaves

Directions:

1   Preheat your grill to 350 to 400 °F. Mix together pepper, chili powder and beef. Split beef mix into four and mold around rounds of goat cheese to create 4 patties. Flavor with pepper and salt. Cook bacon until crisp and then drain using paper towels.
2   Set aside tablespoon bacon drippings to sauté onion and garlic in. Add vinegar, seasonings and preserves. Set aside. Grill patties at 4-5 minutes per side. Serve patties

using toasted buns alongside bacon, onion mixture, peach slices, basil leaves.

BBQ Peach Pulled Slow Cooker Chicken

Ingredients Needed:

- lbs of chicken thighs
- ½ cup of BBQ sauce
- 1 garlic clove
- 2 tbsp of apple cider vinegar
- ½ tsp of paprika
- ½ tsp of chili powder
- 2 peaches
- rice
- cilantro

Directions:

1 Cook chicken using a slow cooker.
2 Mix together vinegar, spices, BBQ sauce, and garlic; stir to combine.
3 Mash peaches.
4 Stir in BBQ sauce and peaches onto the slow cooker.
5 Keep cooking on high for at least 3 hours.
6 When done, shred chicken.
7 Put back chicken onto the crockpot and mix with left over juice.
8 Top rice with the chicken with a sprinkling of cilantro.

Rhubarb Buckwheat Porridge with Green Figs

Ingredients Needed:

Raw buckwheat porridge:

- 1 cup of raw buckwheat groats
- 2-3 cups of water
- 1 tbsp of apple cider vinegar
- ½ cup of almond milk
- ¼ cup of pure maple syrup
- 1 tbsp of almond butter
- 1 tbsp of chia seeds
- ½ tbsp of coconut oil
- 1 tsp of vanilla extract
- ½ tsp of cinnamon
- cardamom

Rhubarb compote:

- 1½ cups of rhubarb
- tbsp of pure maple syrup
- 1 tbsp of water
- ¼ tsp of cardamom

Garnishes:

- green figs
- pepitas

Directions:

1   Soak buckwheat groats in 2 to 3 cups water with apple cider vinegar. Leave overnight in the fridge or for 8 hours.
2   After soaking, strain and rinse well.
3   Using a blender, pulse groats with chia seeds, coconut oil, almond milk, cinnamon, cardamom, almond butter, maple syrup, and vanilla extract,

Rhubarb Compote Prep:

1. Cook together maple syrup, sliced rhubarb, water, and cardamom over medium to high heat for 10 to 12 minutes.
2. Options: The compote can be layered the on the porridge or blend in with buckwheat.
3. After pouring some to glass, top using pepitas and figs.
4. Leave in the fridge if not serving immediately.

Pickled "Fried" Green Tomatoes with Buttermilk-Herb Sauce

Ingredients Needed:

Pickling:

- 1 cup of water
- 1 cup of apple cider vinegar
- tbsp of sugar
- ½ tsp of kosher salt
- 16 green tomato

Tomatoes:

- 5 tbsp of buttermilk
- tbsp of olive oil mayonnaise
- tsp of dill
- 2 tsp of apple cider vinegar
- 1 clove garlic
- ½ tsp of black pepper
- 1¼ cup of panko
- ⅓ cup of masa harina
- ¼ tsp of salt
- 1 egg
- 1 egg white
- ¼ cup of flour
- tbsp of EV olive oil

Directions:

1. Let boil all picking ingredients. Add in the tomatoes and keep cooking for 2 minutes. When done, leave for 15 minutes, drain and pat dry.
2. Mix together next 4 of ingredients up to garlic with 5 tablespoons buttermilk; whisk. Add ¼-teaspoon pepper.
3. Toast panko for 2 minutes. Remove from fire and add ¼-teaspoon salt, masa harina, and ¼-teaspoon pepper. Mix

together egg, egg white, 2 tablespoons buttermilk; stir. Put flour in a separate dish.

4   Coat tomato slices using flour first, dip in the egg mixture, and lastly coat with the panko.

5   Cook half of the tomatoes over medium to high heat until browned. Do the same with the rest of the tomatoes and serve with the sauce.

Easy Duck Carnitas

Ingredients Needed:

- 4 duck legs
- 1 tsp of salt
- 1 tsp of smoked paprika
- 1 tsp of Aleppo pepper
- 1/2 tsp of cumin seed
- 1/2 tsp of Mexican oregano
- 1 navel orange
- 1 cup of water

Directions:

1. Heat oven: 350 degrees.
2. Using an oven-safe pot, Arrange duck legs with the skins-side-up. Season using all the spices and squeeze orange juice over it. Add water and cover.

Let the duck cook (braise) 1 ½ hours. After, remove cover and roast for 1 hour. Shred meat minus the bones and skin when done. Serve with cilantro, wedges and pickled onions.

Cinnamon-Sugar Quinoa Doughnut Holes

Ingredients Needed:

- ½ cup of rice flour
- ½ cup of sorghum flour
- ½ cup of quinoa flour
- 1 tbsp of potato starch
- ½ tsp of guar gum
- 1 tsp baking powder
- 1 tbsp of egg replacer
- ½ tsp of salt
- ½ tsp of cinnamon
- ¼ tsp nutmeg
- 1 ¼ cups of soy milk
- 1 tbsp of apple cider vinegar
- 1 tbsp of camelina oil
- ⅓ cup of coconut sugar
- ⅓ cup of stevia
- 1 cup of quinoa
- 1 tbsp of cinnamon
- ⅓ cup of sugar

Directions:

1. Preheat oven: 350 °F. Pre-grease muffin pan.
2. Combine starch, baking powder flours, guar gum, egg replacer, nutmeg, salt, and cinnamon; whisk.
3. Combine milk, sugar, stevia, vinegar, and oil; whisk. Add in flour mix.
4. Add the quinoa.
5. Bake for 7 to 8 minutes.
6. Mix together cinnamon and coarse sugar.
7. Coat baked muffins with spiced sugar; let cool.

Grilled Zucchini with Toasted Fennel Seed Vinaigrette

Ingredients Needed:

Grilled zucchini:

- 1.5-2 lbs of zucchini
- 1 tbsp of olive oil
- kosher salt
- pepper

Toasted fennel seed vinaigrette:

- tsp of fennel seeds
- tsp of apple cider vinegar
- 2 tbsp of olive oil
- .5 tsp of kosher salt
- .25 tsp of black pepper
- 1 tbsp of flat leaf parsley

Directions:

Zucchini:

1. Cut zucchini in one-fourth inch strips (lengthways) and then coat olive oil.
2. Grill for 2 minutes, making sure to create grill marks. Flavor with salt & pepper.

Vinaigrette:

1. Heat sauté pan, add fennel seeds then cook fennel seeds for around 4 to 5 minutes. Transfer immediately on separate bowl.
2. Stir in the salt, pepper, olive oil, and apple cider vinegar; whisk well.
3. Drizzle grilled zucchini with the vinaigrette. Top with parsley.

Salmon Tacos, Cilantro Slaw and Chipotle Cream

Ingredients Needed:

Salmon:

- 1 1/2 pounds of salmon filets
- oil
- ½ tsp of chili powder
- ½ tsp of cumin
- ½ tsp of paprika
- ½ tsp of oregano
- 1 tsp of salt
- ½ tsp of black pepper

Chipotle crema:

- ½ tsp of chipotle chili powder
- 1 cup of sour cream
- Lime zest
- 1 tbsp of fresh lime juice
- 1 tsp of sugar

Cilantro slaw:

- 2 cups of cabbage
- 1/4 cup of cilantro
- ½ cup of mayonnaise
- tbsp of sugar
- 1 tsp of apple cider vinegar
- Salt
- black pepper

Garnish:

- salsa
- 8 corn tortillas
- avocado
- wedges lime

Directions:

1 Heat grill to 400 °F. Brush racks using oil.
2 Combine chili powder, salt, pepper, oregano, cumin, and paprika. Coat salmon using oil and season with spice mixture.
3 Grill the salmon till seared. Flip after 4 minutes then keep grilling to cook through.
4 Let cool on a plate.
5 Combine the lime zest, chipotle powder, creme fraiche, lime juice, sugar; whisk. Flavor using salt and ground black pepper.
6 Combine apple cider vinegar, sugar, mayonnaise, and flavor using salt & pepper. Mix cilantro and cabbage with the dressing; toss.
7 Using flaked salmon, fill the tortillas and top your salsa of choice, the chipotle lime, and finally with the cabbage. Serve with fresh slices of avocado and lime wedges.

Carne Asada Fries Recipe

Ingredients Needed:

- 1 1/2 lbs of flank steak
- Garlic cloves
- 1 jalapeño pepper
- 1/2 cup of cilantro
- 1/4 cup of olive oil
- 1/3 cup of lime juice
- 1/4 cup of orange juice
- tbsp of apple cider vinegar
- salt
- pepper
- 32 oz french fries

Topping:

- 1/2 cup of sour cream
- 1 cup of guacamole
- 1/2-3/4 cup of pico de gallo

Directions:

1. Combine steak marinade ingredients together. Add in the steak and leave in the fridge for 2 to 4 hours.
2. Discard marinade when done.
3. Grill the flank steak for at least 7 to 9 minutes each side.
4. Slice into small strips, against the grain.
5. Cook fries separately.
6. Put 1-serving full of fries on a dish.
7. Place one-fourth flank strips, topped by pico, guacamole, and sour cream.

Power Breakfast Muffins

Ingredients Needed:

- 1/2 cup of buckwheat flour
- 1/2 cup of oat flour
- 1/4 cup of banana flour
- stevia
- 1 tsp of baking soda
- 1/2 tsp of baking powder
- 1 tsp of cinnamon
- 1/2 tsp of banana extract
- 1/2 tsp of vanilla extract bourbon
- 1 cup of almond milk
- 1/4 cup of banana
- 1/2 cup of blueberries
- 1/4 cup of zucchini
- 1/2 tsp of apple cider vinegar
- 1 tbs flax seed
- 1/4 tsp of coconut

Directions:

1. Preheat the oven: 350 °F.
2. Combine stevia, baking soda, flours, baking powder, flax and cinnamon; whisk well. Add in the almond milk, extracts, banana, apple cider vinegar, blueberries, and zucchini. Whisk well to combine.
3. Pour batter on a pre-greased or paper-lined muffin pan. Put ¼-teaspoon shredded coconut on top of each muffin.
4. Bake for 25 minutes.

Grilled Chicken and White Sauce

Ingredients Needed:

- chicken thighs
- 1 cup of mayonnaise
- 3/4 cup of apple cider vinegar
- 1 tbsp of sugar
- 1 tsp of mustard powder
- zest 1 lemon
- Kosher salt
- black pepper

Directions:

1 Mix together all the BBQ sauce ingredients. Leave in the fridge, covered, for 1 hour.
2 Preheat grill.
3 Flavor chicken using pepper & salt.
4 Grill chicken for about 5-7 minutes each side.
5 Serve using leftover BBQ sauce.

Super Moist Blueberry Corn Muffins with Whipped Maple Butter

Ingredients Needed:

- 1 cup of almond milk
- tsp of apple cider vinegar
- 1 1/2 cups of cornmeal
- 1 1/2 cups of flour
- 2 tsp of cornstarch
- 2 tsp of baking powder
- 1 tsp of baking soda
- 1/2 tsp of salt
- 2/3 cup of vegetable oil
- 2/3 cup of sugar
- 1 1/2 cups of blueberries

Directions:

1. Preheat oven: 350 °F.
2. Combine cider vinegar and almond milk. Set aside.
3. Sift together 1 1/2 cups flour, cornstarch, cornmeal, baking soda, baking powder, and salt.
4. Mix in sugar and oil into almond milk mix.
5. Whisk until frothy before adding dry ingredients.
6. Combine teaspoon flour with the blueberries before adding into the batter.
7. Pour batter into muffin cups close to the top.
8. Bake for 28 to 30 minutes.
9. Let cool for 2 minutes before serving topped with whipped maple butter.

Zephyr Squash, Onion and Apple Saute

Ingredients Needed:

- 1 tbsp of coconut oil
- 1 sweet onion
- salt
- pepper
- 5"-6" zephyr squash
- 1 apple
- 1 tsp of palm sugar
- ¼ cup of vegetable broth
- 2 tsp of apple cider vinegar
- flat leaf parsley

Directions:

1 Using a skillet, melt coconut oil.
2 Cook onion seasoned with salt & pepper until sizzling.
3 Lower heat and cook onions slowly.
4 Stir in apple and squash, flavoring with more pepper and salt. Stir while cooking.
5 Pour vegetable broth with sugar.
6 Simmer while covered over low heat for 5 minutes.
7 Keep cooking till broth has almost evaporated.
8 Season to taste.
9 Toss using 2 teaspoons apple cider vinegar prior to serving.
10 Top with parsley.

Farro Salad

Ingredients Needed:

- 1 cup of farro
- 1/3 cup of apple cider vinegar
- 1 tsp of kosher salt
- bay leaves
- tbsp of olive oil
- 2 tbsp of lemon juice
- 2 cups of arugula leaves
- 1 cup of basil leaves
- 1 cup of mint leaves
- 1 1/2 cups of cherry tomatoes
- 1/2 cup of Parmesan cheese
- 1/2 cup of pistachio nuts
- sea salt

Directions:

1. Simmer faro in 2 and 2/3 cups water, salt, bay leaves and apple cider vinegar for around 30 minutes. Leave to cool when done, removing all bay leaves.
2. Combine lemon juice, salt and olive oil, whisk. Mix in arugula then cooked faro; mix. Add in tomatoes, pistachios and herbs. Optional: add a dash of sea salt and parmesan.

Pineapple Baked Chicken

Ingredients Needed:

- 1 tsp of ginger
- Garlic cloves
- ¼ cup of coconut aminos
- 1 tbsp of apple cider vinegar
- 1 tbsp of honey
- chicken breasts
- 1 cup of pineapple
- onions
- black pepper

Directions:

1 Preheat your oven: 350 °F.
2 Mix coconut aminos, ginger, garlic, apple cider vinegar, and honey. Place breasts of chicken into baking pan and add mixture on top. Arrange slices of pineapple on top.
3 Bake for around 30 to 40 minutes.
4 Prior to serving, put black pepper and onions on top.

Smoked Chicken with Peach Ginger Barbecue Sauce

Ingredients Needed:

Chicken:

- 1 2 to 4 lbs of chicken
- cloves garlic
- 1 tbsp of kosher salt
- 1 tbsp of pepper
- tbsp of canola oil

Peach ginger BBQ sauce:

- peaches
- 1 lemon
- ½ cup of sweet onion
- ¼ cup of apple cider vinegar
- 1 tbsp of canola oil
- tbsp of honey
- tbsp of mustard
- ⅛ tsp of dry mustard
- ⅛ tsp of cumin
- ¼ tsp of kosher salt

Directions:

Chicken Prep:

1. Halve the chicken.
2. Put half of the salt, minced garlic and pepper under the chicken skin.
3. Coat skin lightly using oil prior to applying the rest of the salt, garlic and pepper. Leave in the fridge covered in plastic wrap.
4. Once smoker is ready, arrange chickens skin-side-up. Keep the temp monitored while cooking.

BBQ sauce:

1. Slice peaches after peeling. Coat each sliced peach using lemon juice.
2. Chop peeled onion.
3. Sauté onion until translucent, stir in peaches plus the rest of the ingredients. Let boil slowly.
4. Simmer over low heat for 45 minutes. Puree the cooked peaches prior to putting back into the pot.

Vegan Pasta Salad with Lime

Ingredients Needed:

- 16 oz of shell pasta
- ¼ cup of olive oil
- 1 tbsp of lime juice
- ½ cup of cilantro
- ¾ cup of vegetable broth
- tbsp of apple cider vinegar
- 1 onion
- 2 cups of corn
- 25 plum tomatoes
- 1 cucumber
- salt
- pepper

Directions:

1 Cook the pasta and drain when done. Mix in cilantro, lime juice, olive oil, broth, vinegar. Mix well then let cool.
2 Mix in tomatoes, cucumber, diced onions, and corn,
3 Season with salt & pepper. Top using fresh cilantro.

Sticky Honey Lime Grilled Chicken

Ingredients Needed:

- chicken thighs
- oil

Sauce:

- juice 1 lime
- 1 tbsp of apple cider vinegar
- 1 cup of honey

Rub:

- tsp of chili powder
- 1 1/4 tsp of cumin
- 1 tsp of garlic salt
- 1/4 tsp of pepper
- 1/2 tsp of coriander
- 1/2 tsp of powder onion

Directions:

1. Heat grill to high.
2. Melt honey, vinegar and lime juice on a saucepan. Simmer then set aside.
3. Coat the chicken with a bit of oil. Combine seasonings and coat chicken with it. Grill for 3 to 5 minutes. When done, serve with the remaining sauce.

Apple & Blue Cheese Chicken Salad

Ingredients Needed:

- ⅔ cup Greek yogurt
- tbsp of mustard
- 1 tbsp of honey
- tbsp of apple cider vinegar
- 2 cups chicken
- 1 apple
- ½ cup of blue cheese
- ¼ cup of pepitas
- salt
- pepper

Directions:

1 Combine mustard, Greek yogurt, honey, and vinegar; stir well.
2 Mix in chicken then stir well.
3 Add in the blue cheese, pepitas or nuts and apples.
4 Serve alongside crackers, pita, sandwich, and salad.

Grilled Pork Chops with Peach, Bourbon, Mustard Sauce

Ingredients Needed:

- pork chops
- peaches
- 1 tbsp of brown sugar
- 1 tbsp of smoked paprika
- 1 tsp of onion powder
- tsp of garlic powder
- 1 tbsp of dry mustard
- 1 tbsp of kosher salt
- 1/2 tsp of black pepper
- 2 cups of peach
- 1 cup of apple cider vinegar
- 1/4 cup of bourbon
- Garlic cloves
- tsp of dry mustard
- 3/4 tsp of red pepper flakes

Directions:

1. Combine onion powder, paprika, brown sugar, dry mustard, tablespoon salt, garlic powder, and pepper. Season pork chops using the rub and leave in the fridge for 4 hours or up to 24 hours.
2. Combine vinegar, garlic, bourbon, dry mustard, preserves, red pepper flakes, and salt. Let boil, and then simmer until it thickens. Set aside to cool.
3. Preheat grill.
4. Grill pork chops for around 4 minutes.
5. Flip the chops and baste using sauce. Keep cooking for 3-4 minutes.
6. Let meat rest for at least 5 minutes.

7   Grill peaches. Cover while grilling for 1-2 minutes each side.

8   Serve pork chops and peaches together.

Raspberry Ripple Buckwheat Porridge

Ingredients Needed:

- 1 cup of buckwheat groats
- 1 tbsp of apple cider vinegar
- tbsp of hemp seeds
- ½ cup of milk
- 1 banana
- 1 tbsp of bee pollen
- juice ½ lemon
- ½ tsp of cardamom
- 1 vanilla bean

Raspberry ripple:

- raspberries
- 1 tbsp of maple syrup

Directions:

1 Soak buckwheat overnight using tablespoon of any acidic of choice and warm water. Drain the following morning and rinse thoroughly.
2 Blend together maple syrup and raspberries till of liquid consistency. Set aside 3 to 4 tablespoons puree.
3 Mix in buckwheat groats plus the rest of the ingredients and blend. To sweeten, just season.
4 Assembly: Put some buckwheat porridge onto bowl then add about a tablespoon raspberry puree, and finally sprinkling using bee pollen.

Buffalo Chicken Tacos with a Bleu Cheese Slaw

Ingredients Needed:

Buffalo chicken tacos:

- 24 flour tortillas
- lb chicken thighs
- grilled corn

Buffalo sauce:

- buffalo wing sauce
- 1½ stick butter
- honey

Blue cheese slaw:

- 1 cabbage
- ½ small red pepper
- 1½ cups of blue cheese dressing
- 1 tbsp of apple cider vinegar
- 1 tsp of sea salt
- ½ tsp of black pepper

Homemade blue cheese dressing:

- oz of blue cheese
- 1 cup of sour cream
- 1 cup of mayonnaise
- ¼ cup of buttermilk
- ¼ tsp of granulated onion
- ½ tsp of salt
- ¼ tsp of black pepper

Directions:

Buffalo Sauce Prep:

1 Melt butter over heat before adding in the honey.

2   Mix hot sauce then blend well with the honey/butter mixture.

3   Set aside after.

Prep for Dressing:

1   Pulse together Greek yogurt or sour cream, half of the bleu cheese and milk mixture till bleu cheese becomes well incorporated.

2   Add into the mayonnaise along with the rest of bleu cheese crumbles plus the seasonings.

3   This dressing tastes best after letting sit for 48 hours.

Prep for the Slaw:

1   Combine vinegar, sea salt, cheese dressing, and pepper. Blend well together.

2   Combine cheese dressing and cabbage mixture; mix well then leave for 4 to 6 hours.

3   Store in the fridge.

Whole-Wheat Waffles

Ingredients Needed:

- 3/4 cup of flour
- 1 tsp baking soda
- 1/4 cup of cornstarch
- 1/2 tsp baking powder
- 1 tsp sugar
- 1/4 tsp salt
- 1 to 1 1/4 cups of milk
- 1 egg
- 1/4 cup of oil
- 1 tsp of vanilla
- 1 tbsp of apple cider vinegar

Directions:

1. Let your waffle iron preheat.
2. Mix together the dry ingredients.
3. Mix egg, vanilla, milk, oil; blend well.
4. Prior to pouring batter into the waffle iron, pour vinegar; stir. Cook waffles based on your waffle iron's specifications.
5. Let cool using a rack when done.

Couscous Kale Salad

Ingredients Needed:

- kale
- 1/3 cup of couscous
- 1 tsp of olive oil
- 1 mango
- 1 small red pepper
- 1 can black beans
- 1/4 cup of sunflower seeds

Dressing:

- olive oil
- 1/4 cup of lemon juice
- 1 and 1/2 tbsp of apple cider vinegar
- 3/4 tbsp of honey
- 1 tsp of dijon
- Salt
- pepper

Directions:

1. Wash and massage kale using cold water then chop then measure five cups before rinsing again. Let dry.
2. Prep the couscous using olive oil and water.
3. Chop mango after peeling and removing pit. Discard red pepper stems then the seeds prior to chopping.
4. Rinse black beans after draining.
5. Combine all dressing ingredients inside a re-sealable jar. Shake well to combine. Drizzle some on the prepped kale.
6. Massage dressing to kale.
7. Add in red pepper, black beans and mango.
8. Prior to serving, add sunflower seeds.

No Fry Firecracker Chicken

Ingredients Needed:

- chicken breasts
- 1 tbsp of olive oil
- Garlic cloves
- 1/4 cup of apple cider vinegar
- 1 cup of brown sugar
- 1/3 cup of ketchup
- tbsp of chili sauce
- tbsp of hot Sauce
- 1/4 tsp of salt
- 1/4 tsp of pepper
- 1 stalk green onion

Directions:

1 Cook garlic using olive oil at low heat for around 30 seconds then add diced chicken and keep cooking.
2 Pour hot sauce, chili sauce and apple cider vinegar. Mix chicken with the sauce. Add brown sugar and keep cooking for at least 10 minutes. Add the salt, pepper and ketchup; stir well. Keep cooking for 20 minutes using low heat. Serve with spring onions and rice.

Caprese Chicken and Basil Vinaigrette

Ingredients Needed:

- 1-1/2 cups of balsamic vinegar
- chicken breasts
- salt
- pepper
- 1 pint of cherry tomatoes
- 8oz of mozzarella pearls

Marinade:

- 1/2 cup of basil
- tbsp of apple cider vinegar
- 1 tbsp of honey
- garlic clove
- salt
- pepper
- 1/2 cup of EV olive oil

Directions:

1   Let boil vinegar. Simmer for 15 to 20 minutes over low heat till it becomes thinner. Leave to cool.
2   Vinaigrette/Marinade Prep: combine all ingredients in the blender minus the olive oil. Pulse so that the garlic and basil are chopped roughly. Gently pour oil in a thin, steady stream.
3   Flavor breasts on each side using pepper and salt & pepper, place inside a Ziploc bag and add in half the marinade. Leave in the fridge for a min of 15 minutes and a max of 4 hours.
4   Mix together mozzarella pearls and cherry tomatoes then toss with the other half of the marinade.

5   Grill chicken for about 3 to 4 minutes each side. Serve topped with the mozzarella and cherry tomato salad plus some vinegar.

Fiery Roasted Brussels Sprouts

Ingredients Needed:

- brussels sprouts
- 3 red jalapeño chilies
- cooking fat
- 1 tsp of salt
- Cloves garlic
- 1 tbsp of apple cider vinegar
- ⅓ cup of walnuts
- 1 tbsp of blackstrap molasses

Directions:

1. Preheat your oven: 400 °F.
2. Halve brussels sprouts in and then cut jalapeño chilies lengthwise. Set aside chili for garnishing.
3. Toss chilies and brussels using cooking fat. Arrange on roasting dish and season with salt.
4. Slice garlic and soak using apple cider vinegar.
5. Bake at for 25 minutes at 400 °F.
6. Add vinegar, walnuts and garlic. Bake for 10 minutes.
7. Add the molasses.

Barbecued Brisket

Ingredients Needed:

- brisket

Rub:

- 1 ½ tsp of paprika
- 1 ½ tsp of onion powder
- 1 tsp of salt
- tsp of salt
- 1 tsp of black pepper
- ¼ cup of brown sugar
- 1 ½ tsp of garlic salt

Baking liquid:

- 1 cup of apple juice
- ½ cup of apple cider vinegar
- 1 cup of BBQ sauce

Directions:

1. Mix seasonings and spices. Season brisket; chill overnight.
2. Grill for 6 to 7 hours at 325.
3. Let stand 15 minutes. Prior to placing into baking dish, carve against grain, and pour a cup apple juice, half-cup apple cider vinegar, and a cup bbq sauce. Use a tin foil to cover well, then bake for 2 to 3 hours more. at 275.
4. Serve while hot.

Blackberry Cupcakes

Ingredients Needed:

- tbsp of butter
- 1/2 cup sugar
- eggs
- 1 tbsp of apple cider vinegar
- tbsp of almond milk
- 1 tsp of vanilla extract
- 1/3 cup of sour cream
- 1 tsp of baking soda
- 1/2 tbsp of cinnamon
- 1/4 tsp cloves
- 1/2 tsp allspice
- 1/2 cup of blackberry jam
- 1-1/2 cups of flour
- 1/4 tsp salt

Blackberry buttercream:

- butter
- 1/2 cup of blackberry jam
- crisco shortening
- 3-4 cups of powdered sugar

Directions:

1. Pre-heat your oven: 350 degrees. Combine almond milk, sour cream and vinegar. Set aside. Combine dry ingredients; set aside.
2. Cream sugar and butter. Add eggs. Add vanilla extract.
3. Alternately mix together flour and buttermilk mixture. Add in half-cup of blackberry jam then scoop 1/3-cup batter onto cupcake cups (yields 12) Bake 20 to 23 minutes. Let cool.

4   For frosting: cream the shortening and butter together. Blend in 3 cups powdered sugar. Add blackberry jam. Add vanilla extract.

Conclusion

Though the natural healing claims of vinegar all throughout the centuries has been varied and plentiful, newly recognized medical benefits of vinegar continue to emerge. Over all, apple cider vinegar is viewed as the ultimate disease-fighting and health-boosting hoe remedy. Most importantly, vinegar has now been known as a potential healer of most of today's common yet serious ailments.

Moreover, adding to the health benefits of apple, a substance called malic acid is formed during the fermentation process of an apple cider vinegar. Malic acid then is the reason why the apple cider vinegar is laced with additional antiviral, antifungal and antibacterial properties.

In a nutshell, apple cider vinegar can be such a big help in revolutionizing your personal health.

Printed in Great Britain
by Amazon.co.uk, Ltd.,
Marston Gate.